Italian Interior Design

Italian Interiors 1990–1999
Italienische Interieurs 1990–1999

Edited by/Herausgegeben von:
Laura Andreini
Nicola Flora
Paolo Giardiello
Gennaro Postiglione

For this edition:
© 2001 teNeues Verlag GmbH + Co KG, Kempen

For the original edition:
© 1999 Federico Motta Editore SpA, Milan

© of the authors for the photographs
cover: Achilli Ghizzardi Associati

Original book title: Case d'autore. Interni italiani 1990 – 1999

English translation: Nina Taranto
German translation: Margot Zander
Production: content publishing, Munich

Published in the US and Canada by teNeues Publishing Company
16 West 22nd Street, New York, N.Y. 10010, USA
Tel.: 001-212-627-9090, Fax: 001-212-627-9511

Published in Germany by teNeues Verlag GmbH + Co KG
Am Selder 37, 47906 Kempen, Germany
Tel.: +49-(0)2152-916-0, Fax: +49-(0)2152-916-111

Published in the UK and Ireland by teNeues Publishing UK Ltd.
77 The London Fruit & Wool Exchange, Brushfield Street, London El 6EP, UK
Tel.: +44-(0)20-7655-0999, Fax: +44-(0)20-7655-0888

www.teneues.com

Die Deutsche Bibliothek – CIP-Einheitsaufnahme
Ein Titeldatensatz für diese Publikation ist bei der Deutschen Bibliothek erhältlich.

ISBN 3-8238-5495-X
Printed in Italy.

contents
inhalt

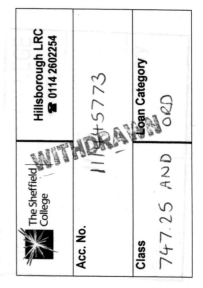

This book is partly self-explanatory; a quick leaf through the pages gives us an idea of the contents – a collection of interior designs in Italy in the last ten years. But it is not only that, and perhaps these notes can offer a better idea of how and why it was put together.
So let's begin with why we decided on Italian Interior Designs and why only in Italy in the last ten years.
First of all, let's look at the term "designer" as it could be misleading. In recent years we have heard a lot about "design" architecture, about recognising the stylistic feature of the designer, about a star system that is promoted more by the name of the designer than by the quality of the work. We are not at all interested in that world – here the term "designer" is used for completely different reasons.
We simply wanted to use this expression to show that behind the definition of an area to live in lies the presence of a perceptive artist. In fact, all too often we are misled into believing that the organisation of an interior must be entrusted to the skill and taste of whoever lives there, or more simply to the slow subsidence of circumstances and necessities that sooner or later outline the shape of the places we live in. This schematic vision reserves for architecture, with a capital A, "more extensive and nobler" interests that involve the urban area. However, we believe that all architecture must be conceived starting from the person who will live in it, based on what will take place inside it, keeping well in mind what that space must represent in the life of that person.
By accentuating the presence of an artist who "designs" and takes into account the character and morphological definition of the parts that make up the interior space of the design, we can give back dignity and importance to a practice of designing; this has been partly

appropriated, or worse, considered by some, as concerning other professionals, not architects. "Designer homes" then, insomuch as they are the result of a precise organisational will and overall arrangement of an artist whose sole interest is to harmoniously combine practical needs with expectations that belong to the nature of whoever will use the areas; technological necessities with evocative potential of the form and materials.

So it is no accident that alongside famous names in the Italian architectural world we find more or less well known young designers. We did not want to consider the career of the individuals, their previous works, the size or financial resources of the client – what we tried to stress was a true consistency between the finished product and the design prerequisites; between constraints and the ability to turn them into incentives for the work; between individual needs and the possibility of influencing a wider social context, between bureaucratic restrictions and freedom of form. This is why the result is not strictly uniform, in other words, we did not favour one stylistic feature over another. Instead, works that are similar in their expressive capacity, even though they look different, appear in strict alphabetical order.

In this sense, we can also justify the total absence of a comment on each work, which would have required separate comparisons, judgements and remarks.

An other term, which it is appropriate to reflect on, is the word "interior", which is basically the reason for the entire study as well as being part of the title.

By interior we did not want to identify a place, in other words define a physically recognisable area, but rather we intended to stress a peculiarity of architecture that for us is indisputable.

Many great architects who have undertaken to teach interior design in Italian universities, often resort to a subtle play on words in Italian to define this design area. Rather than "interior design", they prefer to talk about "design viewed from inside", thus emphasising not a different area but only a movement of the observation point from which to begin outlining the design.

Of course, in English the term "interior design" is a broader definition that other languages do not completely reflect and can be translated as both "inside" and "interior", and it is the latter that gives us a better understanding of the aspect that interests us most. By definition, interior is everything relating to a spatially or imaginarily enclosed area, often in direct reference to spiritual facts and individual awareness. With this there is no longer any doubt that, together with satisfying physical and practical needs, design constructs spaces where man can impose needs of a psychological, emotional and cognitive nature. The construction of an interior space is the definition of an open narrative plot inside which all the protagonists can freely construct the individual profile of their own character. It is a showcase where each object can evoke reminiscences, histories – in a single word, memories.

Last but not least, a final mention of the decision to limit the field to Italy in the last decade. After the great period of architecture following World War II, when the interior design methods defined a scenario consistent with social and economic expectations, Italy was the centre of important and contradictory research. Behind the labels set by critics such as radical, postmodern, neo-modern, minimalism, etc... are hidden in reality comparatively individual adventures that correspond to precise lines of experimentation and research.

But these cultural manifestations (as already described in recent histories of architecture, décor and design that tried to bring order to the period from the Sixties to the Eighties), are already part of the history of the discipline, linked to times and fashions that burnt out quickly by concentrating on prestige. This last decade, this tail end of the millennium that we are still inhabiting, even now affects us too closely and since it lacks a long history, cannot be defined using frames of reference that belong to the critics of the sector. Unpublished experiences now appear beside the shapes and trends of previous years, trying to satisfy the many and changing requests of the client. In our opinion, because of our involvement, we can only represent this accumulation of styles and idioms by presenting it, without making any judgements or declaring any goals.
All the published designs represent the multi-coloured and fragmented face of our times; some already show the signs of "something that was and is to some extent no longer", others, on the other hand, may foreshadow scenarios that we will discuss in future years. Without doubt, they testify to the effort of designers who, in very difficult working conditions, wholeheartedly implement slow, widespread change, beginning not with the most striking manifestations, but by working on the most intimate foundation, the interior of our everyday life.

A.F.G.P.

Bereits auf den ersten Blick erschließt sich der Inhalt dieses Buches: Innenarchitektur, die in den letzten zehn Jahren in Italien entstand. Das ist jedoch längst nicht alles. Die folgenden Zeilen sollen die Kriterien erläutern, nach denen das Buch zusammengestellt wurde.

Beginnen wir zunächst mit der Klärung der Bezeichnung „Innenarchitekt". In den letzten Jahren wurde viel Aufhebens um eine Innenarchitektur gemacht, die die Handschrift ihres Gestalters trägt, es ging um die Erkennbarkeit bestimmter Formensprachen und man huldigte einer Szene von Stars, die sich eher über Namen als über die Qualität ihrer Werke definiert. All dies liegt unseren Absichten fern. Die Bezeichnung „Innenarchitekt" wird hier aus ganz anderen Gründen verwendet. Uns liegt daran zu verdeutlichen, dass sich hinter der Definition eines Wohnraumes ein Künstler verbirgt, der sich dieser Rolle auch bewusst ist. Allzu oft ist man verleitet zu glauben, dass die Organisation eines Raumes von den Mitteln und Vorstellungen seiner Bewohner abhänge. Bisweilen korrespondiert dies mit einer Defintion von Architektur, die dieser „höhere und edlere" Interessen in Hinblick auf die Gestaltung des urbanen Raumes zuspricht.

Wir hingegen sind der Meinung, dass jede Architektur vom Standpunkt derjenigen aus erdacht werden muss, die in ihr leben. Die Tätigkeiten, die in ihr verrichtet werden, sowie eine klare Vorstellung, was dieser Raum im Leben des Menschen repräsentiert, sollten im Vordergrund stehen. Das Wirken eines Künstlers hervorzuheben, der die Gestaltung des Inneren der Architektur „plant", bedeutet, einer Art des Planens wieder Würde zu verleihen, die zum Teil nicht mehr praktiziert wird. „Designerhäuser" sind somit als Orte zu verstehen, die das Ergebnis exakter organisatorischer Erwägungen sind. Sie sind die komplexe Inszenierung eines Künstlers, dessen Interesse vornehmlich darin besteht, praktische Anforderungen mit den Erwartungen der Bewohner in Einklang zu bringen. Außerdem geht es um die Verbindung technologischer Vorgaben mit evokativen Formen und Materialien.

Unter diesem Gesichtspunkt ist es also kein Zufall, dass neben etablierten Namen der italienischen Innenarchitekturszene auch einige jüngere Vertreter zu finden sind, die mehr oder weniger bekannt sind. Die Karrieren der einzelnen Künstler, ihre früheren Werke sowie Umfeld und finanzielle Mittel der Klienten sind nicht Gegenstand dieses Buches. Es soll vielmehr der Versuch gemacht werden, engere Zusammenhänge hervorzuheben: zwischen der vollendeten Gestaltung und den Voraussetzungen des Projekts, zwischen Einschränkungen und der Fähigkeit, diese zugunsten des Werkes umzuformen, zwischen den Bedürfnissen des Einzelnen und der Möglichkeit, in einen weiteren sozialen Kontext einzugreifen, zwischen behördlichen Auflagen und der Freiheit der gebauten Form. Aus diesem Grund ist das Ergebnis nicht unbedingt homogen. Es wurde kein Stil bevorzugt. Die Auflistung der Werke, die sich in ihrer Ausdruckskraft ähneln, in ihrem Aussehen jedoch unterscheiden, erfolgt in streng alphabetischer Reihenfolge.

In diesem Sinne ist auch das Fehlen von jeglichen Kommentaren zu sehen, die unweigerlich zu Bewertungen und einseitigen Urteilen geführt hätten.

Ein anderer Begriff, über den es sich nachzudenken lohnt, ist das „Interieur", das letztendlich den Anstoß zu diesem Werk lieferte und deshalb mehr als ein einfacher Untertitel ist. Es war nicht unsere Absicht, mit dem Interieur einen physisch abgegrenzten Raum festzulegen, sondern vielmehr eine Besonderheit der Innenarchitektur zu unterstreichen.

Viele große Architekten, die sich der Herausforderung gestellt haben, Innenarchitektur an italienischen Fakultäten für Architektur zu lehren, haben sich zur besseren Definition oft eines subtilen Wortspiels bedient. Statt von „Innenarchitektur" sprachen sie lieber von einer „Architektur, die von innen heraus gesehen wird". Damit betonten sie keinen anderen Fachbereich, sondern verschoben lediglich die Perspektive, aus der sich ein Projekt zu entwickeln beginnt. Im Englischen wird dieser Bereich als „Interior Design" bezeichnet, und die Bedeutung dieses Ausdrucks lässt leichter auf die Inhalte rückschließen als es die Übersetzung in anderen Sprachen zulässt. „Interior" kann man sowohl mit „innen" als auch mit „innwendig" übersetzen. Genau dieser letztgenannte Ausdruck, der nur selten in Verbindung mit Architektur genannt wird, lässt jenen Aspekt erahnen, der uns am meisten interessiert. Der Definition nach steht „innwendig" für alles, was räumlich oder geistig abgrenzbar ist. Damit ist zweifellos bewiesen, dass die Architektur, neben der Erfüllung praktischer Anforderungen, Räume schafft, die den emotionalen Bedürfnissen des Menschen entsprechen. Die Schaffung eines Innenraums ist vergleichbar mit einer offenen Erzählung, in der jeder Protagonist das individuelle Profil seiner eigenen Persönlichkeit frei festlegen kann.

Zuletzt noch eine Anmerkung zu der Entscheidung, das Thema auf italienische Projekte des letzten Jahrzehnts zu beschränken.

In der Nachkriegszeit wurden in Italien im Bereich der Innenarchitektur Projektmethoden entwickelt, die einen Zusammenhang zwischen sozialen und wirtschaftlichen Erwartungen definierten. Italien wurde zum Zentrum wichtiger und zugleich widersprüchlicher Forschungserfahrungen. Hinter Schlagworten wie *radical*, post-modern, neo-modern, Minimalismus etc., die von der Kritik geprägt wurden, verbergen sich in Wirklichkeit mehr oder weniger individuelle Erfahrungen, die klaren Strömungen in der experimentellen Architektur und in der Forschung entsprechen.

Die jüngsten Abhandlungen über Architektur, Einrichtung oder Design, in denen versucht wird, die Zeit der 1960er- bis 1980er-Jahre zu ordnen, zeigen jedoch bereits, dass solche Äußerungen bereits Teil der Geschichte sind und an Zeiten und Moden anknüpfen, die sich schnell erschöpfen. Wir erleben diesen letzten Abschnitt des Jahrtausends allerdings noch aus zu großer Nähe, und in Ermangelung jener historischen Perspektive lässt sich dieser Zeitraum nicht mit den üblichen Paradigmen der Kritik einordnen.

Zu den Strömungen der vergangenen Jahre gesellen sich bislang unbekannte Erfahrungswerte, mit denen man versucht, den unterschiedlichsten Wünschen der heutigen Auftraggeber gerecht zu werden.

Unserer Meinung nach kann man eine solche Vielfalt an Stilen nur darstellen, indem man sie zeigt, wobei von Beurteilungen Abstand genommen werden muss.

Alle veröffentlichten Projekte spiegeln in ihrer Gesamtheit das bunte und zersplitterte Bild unserer Zeit. Einige tragen bereits die Zeichen von „etwas, das gewesen ist und zum Teil nicht mehr ist". Andere hingegen nehmen vielleicht Inhalte vorweg, die Gegenstand zukünftiger Diskussionen sein werden. In jedem Fall legen sie Zeugnis über das Schaffen von Architekten ab, die unter schwierigsten Bedingungen dank ihres konstanten Einsatzes einen langsamen und weitläufigen Umbruch einleiten. Ein Umbruch, der seinen Ursprung im intimsten Bereich überhaupt hat, nämlich in unserem Alltag.

A.F.G.P.

11

Italian Interior Design

Italian Interiors 1990–1999
Italienische Interieurs 1990–1999

14

Casa Bardazzi
Prato, 1995
collaborator/mitarbeiter:
Lucia Di Blasi
photographer/fotograf:
Alessandro Ciampi

ansari

22

House/Haus in Costa San Giorgio
Florence/Florenz, 1992
collaborator/mitarbeiter:
Michael Heffernan
photographer/fotograf:
Alessandro Ciampi

archea

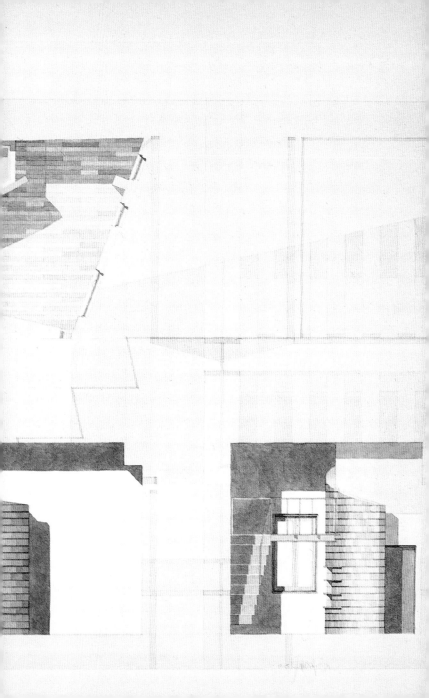

36

Villa in Lurago Marinone
Como, 1994–1995
collaborators/mitarbeiter:
Patricia Viel
Francesca Simen
photographer/fotograf:
Gionata Xerra

citterio dwan

48

Restoration in Mantova/
Restaurierung in Mantua,
1996
collaborators/mitarbeiter:
Corrado Anselmi
Antonia Pintus
photographer/fotograf:
Santi Caleca

cordero

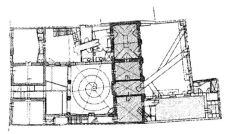

62

Detached family house/
Einfamilienhaus
Langhirano, Parma, 1991
photographers/fotografen:
Davoli and/und Buzzoni

cortesi

76

Casa Gino Battista
Triggiano, Bari, 1986–1992
collaborators/mitarbeiter:
Gino Battista
Nicola Settanni
Vito Borbone
Onofrio D'Anghia
photographer/fotograf:
Sergio Riccio

dalisi

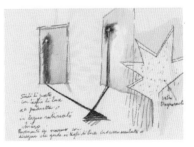

88

Casa Romeo-Caminiti
Varano, Ancona, 1998–1999
collaborator/mitarbeiter:
Alberto Colzani
photographer/fotograf:
Mac Zambelli

deganello

98

Detached family house/
Einfamilienhaus
Blera, Viterbo, 1995
collaborators/mitarbeiter:
Gregory Bordynoswki
Key Inoue
photographer/fotograf:
Santi Caleca

di franco

110

Casa Mordini-Reginato
Florence/Florenz, 1998
photographer/fotograf:
Fabio Fabbrizzi

fabbrizzi

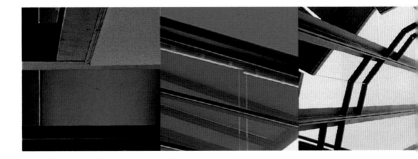

118

The one and the other face/
Das eine und das andere Gesicht
Legnano, Milan/Mailand, 1991–1996
collaborators/mitarbeiter:
Ifka Giller
Maurizio Passaretta
Dario Saita
photographer/fotograf:
Santi Caleca

ferrario

128

Casa Romolo Nardi
Sant'Antimo, Naples/Neapel,
1995–1999
collaborators/mitarbeiter:
Paolo Errico
Luca Mosele
photographer/fotograf:
Rino Giardiello

fgp studio di architettura

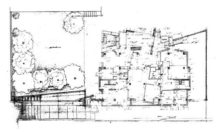

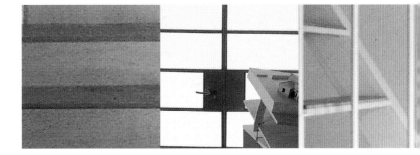

140

House of the architect on
piazza Gesù e Maria/
Haus des Architekten an
der piazza Gesù e Maria
Naples/Neapel, 1992–1993
photographer/fotograf:
Sergio Ricci

fiocco raffone

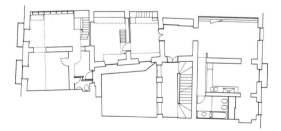

152

House in Naples/
Haus in Neapel,
1997–1998
collaborator/mitarbeiter:
Simona Ottieri
photographer/fotograf:
Peppe Maisto

gambardella

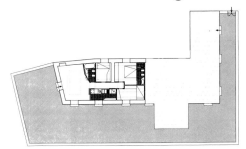

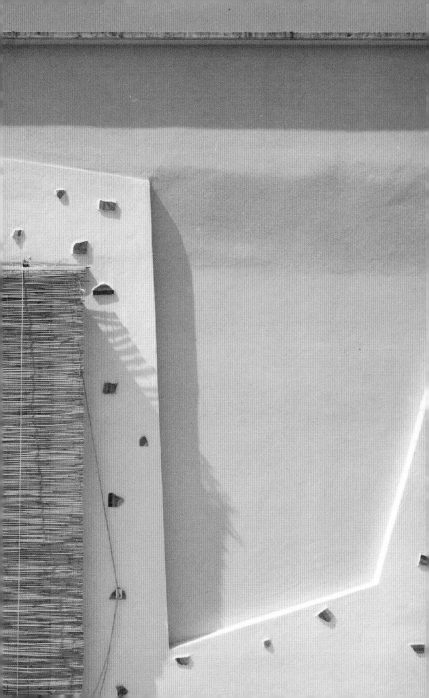

162

Casa Nicosia
Vittoria, Ragusa, 1995–1998
photographer/fotograf:
Santi Caleca

grasso cannizzo

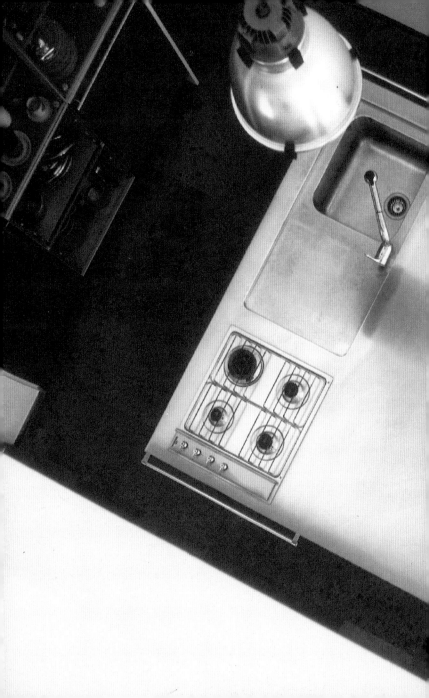

172

Apartment and studio
of a rock musician/
Apartment und Studio eines
Rockmusikers
Fiesole, Florence/Florenz,
1997
collaborator/mitarbeiter:
Beatrice Fei
photographer/fotograf:
Alessandro Ciampi

greppi

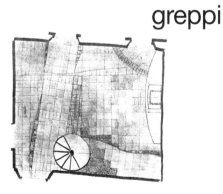

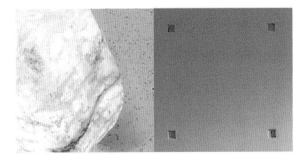

182

House/Haus in Prato,
1996
photographer/fotograf:
Alessandro Ciampi

guerrini

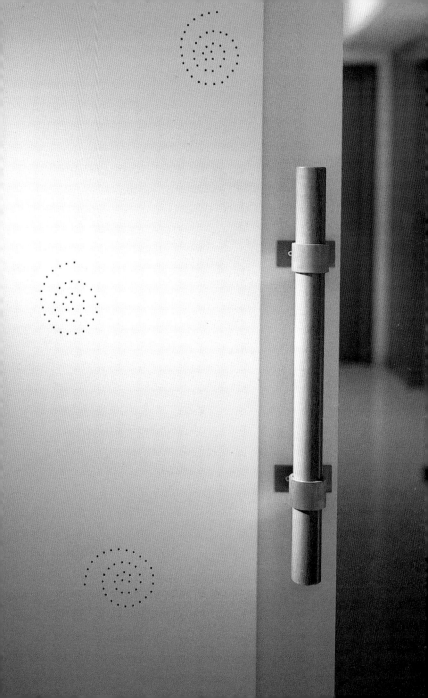

192

Casa Balbarini
Pisa, 1989
photographer/fotograf:
Mario Ciampi

ioli carmassi

206

House in via Ettore Ximenes/
Haus in der via Ettore Ximenes
Rome/Roma, 1996–1998
photographer/fotograf:
Roberto Bossaglia

laudani

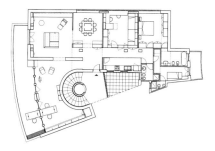

218

Casa Daolio
Guastalla, Reggio Emilia, 1989–1995
collaborator/mitarbeiter:
Piervittorio Prevedello
photographer/fotograf:
Dida Biggi

lombardo scarpa scarpa

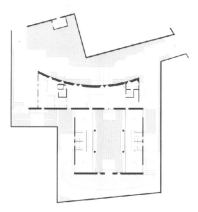

228

House for two young couples/
Haus für zwei junge Paare
Filottrano, Ancona, 1995–1998
photographer/fotograf:
Alessandro Ciampi

luccioni

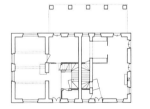

238

Showroom Bisazza
New York, 1998
collaborators/mitarbeiter:
B. Gregori
E. Morra
photographer/fotograf:
Alberto Ferrero

mendini

Renovation in Florence/
Umbau in Florenz,
1989–1991
collaborator/mitarbeiter:
Fabrizio Fabietti
photographer/fotograf:
Arrigo Coppitz

michelizzi

248

258

Apartment on piazza
Postierla/Apartment an
der piazza Postierla
Siena, 1994–1997
photographer/fotograf:
Paola De Pietri

milani

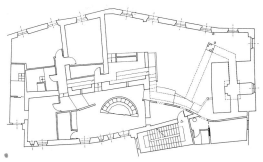

272

Farmhouse/Bauernhaus
Lastra a Signa, Florence/
Florenz, 1998
collaborators/mitarbeiter:
Francesca Cei
Bettina Gelli
Elisabetta Grassi
photographer/fotograf:
Pietro Savorelli

nardi

284

Casa M. F.
Caltagirone, Catania, 1996–1998
photographer/fotograf:
Salvatore Gozzo

navarra

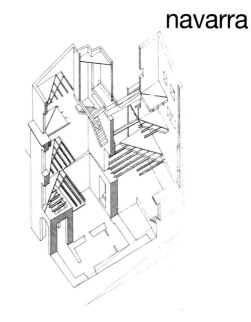

296

House/Haus in Bari,
1997–1998
collaborators/mitarbeiter:
Paolo A.M. Maffiola
Vito Primavera
photographer/fotograf:
Alberto Muciaccia

netti associati

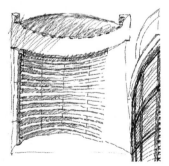

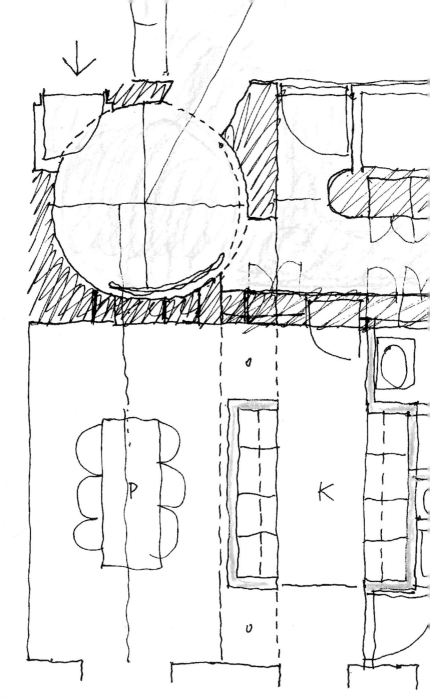

P

K

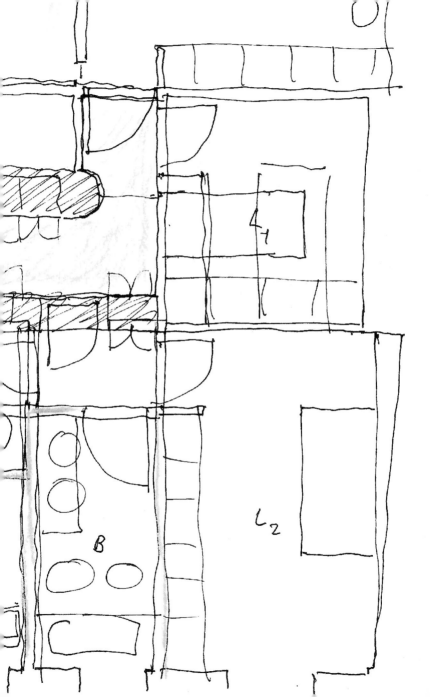

306

House in via Balilla/
Haus in der via Balilla
Forte dei Marmi, Lucca, 1995–1996
photographer/fotograf:
Mario Ciampi

pellegrini

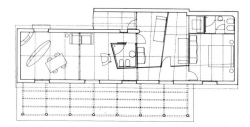

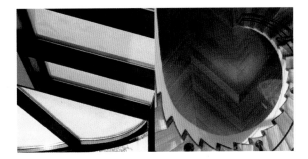

316

House/Haus in Rho,
Milan/Mailand, 1985–1987
photographer/fotograf:
Alberto Piovano

peracchio

326

Casa Borea-Lombardi
San Remo, Imperia, 1995–1998
collaborator/mitarbeiter:
Massimo Noceto
photographer/fotograf:
Alberto Piovano

romanelli

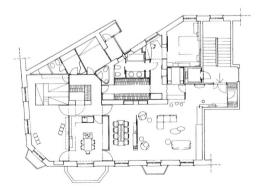

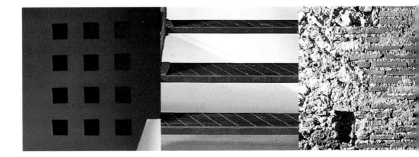

338

Interior/Interieur
L'Aquila, 1995
collaborator/mitarbeiter:
Patrizia Leone
photographer/fotograf:
Alberto Muciaccia

scaglione

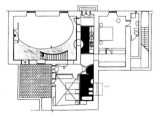

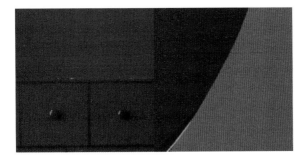

346

Casa Greer
London, 1993–1994
collaborators/mitarbeiter:
Federica Barbiero
Gerard Taylor
photographer/fotograf:
Santi Caleca

sottsass associati

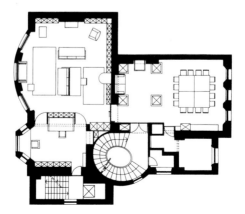

356

Casa Turchi
Falconara, Ancona, 1984–1986
photographer/fotograf:
Alessandro Ciampi

turchi

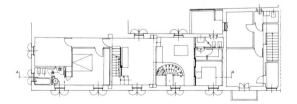

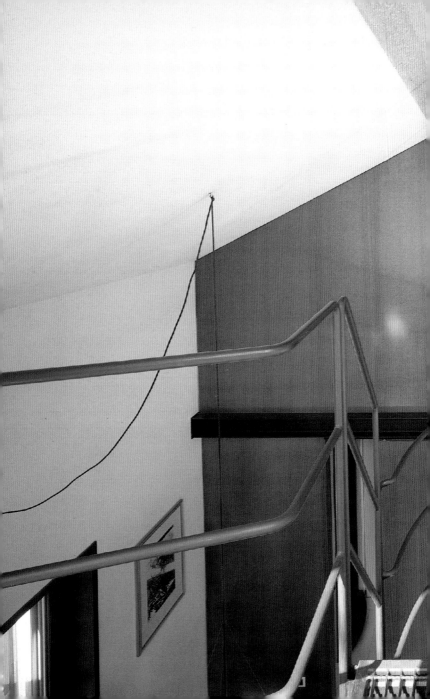

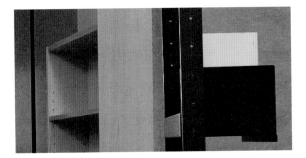

Casa Valbusa
Verona, 1995
photographer/fotograf:
A. Garuti

valentini

376

Villa in Verona,
1991
photographer/fotograf:
Marcato – Studio Wald

vigo

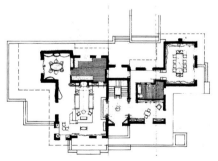